FROM MY KITCHEN TO YOURS

ESTHER JOSEPH SAMUEL

ISBN 978-93-5610-231-6
© ESTHER JOSEPH SAMUEL 2022
Published in India 2022 by Pencil

A brand of

One Point Six Technologies Pvt. Ltd.
123, Building J2, Shram Seva Premises,
Wadala Truck Terminal, Wadala (E)
Mumbai 400037, Maharashtra, INDIA
E connect@thepencilapp.com
W www.thepencilapp.com

Author biography

ESTHER SAMUEL, the person who loves her KITCHEN; her favourite place in her home. Cooking and experimenting on food has always been a passion for the author, who has tried and tested many dishes. She believes cooking to be a stress reliever. She is known for her quick and easy to make vegetarian recipes. She shares simple recipes, good for beginners as well as active cooks. Her work is easy to understand and follow, due to the use of common cookery terms and also certain tips which she shares, as an extra guide. She makes an effort in developing a taste for vegetarian dishes for all, young and old.

She wants to pass on this 'legacy' to the world. Esther Samuel's Kitchen is always ready to serve more and better. Esther's love for food is seen in the recipes, she makes and shares. She has already authored five recipe books and has thrice been on cookery shows on television.

CONTENTS

Epigraph

"GOOD FOOD IS GOOD MOOD"

Preface

This book- FROM MY KITCHEN TO YOURS- is a compilation of simple, quick and easy to make, vegetarian Indian recipes. The readers will find that all the ingredients used in the recipes are easily available and the glossary will also help with the Indian terminology. The language used is easy to understand the method too. Also the tips and other information shared in the book will serve as a fruitful guide to the readers. This book is apt for beginners as well as active cooks as it will help them make and serve better.

Acknowledgements

BOOK DEDICATED TO:

- THE ALMIGHTY, whose unlimited blessings has made it possible for me to reach all of you.

- My family, my friends and all my well-wishers who have always gone out of their way to co-operate and support me, at any point of time.

- A very big and special thank you to all those who have encouraged me and been a motivating factor always.

- I also take this opportunity to thank all my readers who always demand for more, from my side and thus boost up my confidence.

EASY TRAVEL CAKE- Perfect for High-tea too.

Ingredients: 60gms maida

125ml milk

60 gms almond slivers (30gms in the cake & 30gm on top)

100gms butter (at room temperature)

200gms condensed milk

70gms almond powder

60gms mix fruit jam

1tsp baking powder

Method: 1) In a bowl, whisk butter and condensed milk till a little fluffy.

2) Add the maida with the baking powder, gradually, and keep

mixing in one direction only.

3) Now add the almond powder, half of the almond slivers and jam.

4) Mix well and pour into a greased cake tin.

5) Spread the remaining half of the almond slivers on the poured mixture.

6) Bake for 25 minutes at 180°C, in a pre-heated oven.

Note: This cake will not rise much but it can be easily stored in the fridge for 15 days.

MIXED VEGETABLE BAKED DISH-SUPER DUPER HIT

Ingredients: 4 slices pineapple

200 gms mixed vegetables (potatoes, French beans, carrots

and green peas)

2 cups white sauce

100 gms boiled macaroni

100 gms boiled spaghetti

1 tsp sugar

2 – 3 cubes cheese

½ cup bread crumbs

Method: 1) Boil the vegetables and mix with boiled macaroni and spaghetti.

2) Add white sauce to it along with sugar and salt. Mix well.

3) Transfer to a greased bake-dish and spread cheese and bread crumbs on it.

4) Bake in a pre-heated oven till the cheese melts at 180° C.

5) Serve hot.

OPEN TOAST- MY FAVOURITE

Ingredients: 3 bread slices

1 cup shredded cheese

2 tblsp tomato ketchup

2 cups white sauce

2 big potatoes (boiled)

½ cup green peas (boiled)

3 tblsp butter

½ cup coriander leaves

Salt to taste

Pepper to taste

½ tsp oregano

½ tsp chilli flakes

Method: 1) Mash the potatoes and peas, mix and keep aside.

2) Now cut the bread slices into 2 and apply butter on each one.

3) Now add coriander leaves, salt, pepper, oregano and chilli flakes to it and mix well.

4) Now apply the mixture on each slice of bread.

5) Now add cheese on it and toast it in an oven.

6) When cheese melts and bread is toasted remove.

7) Garnish with tomato ketchup and serve.

SIMPLE SPAGHETTI- SUPER EASY

Ingredients: 1 cup boiled spaghetti with little salt

1 cup shredded cheese

½ cup tomato ketchup

2 cups white sauce

Method: 1) Take a bowl and mix the spaghetti and white sauce.

2) Put it in a greased dish and sprinkle cheese on it.

3) Also put tomato ketchup over it.

4) Bake in a pre-heated oven till the cheese melts.

5) Serve hot.

BAKED MACARONI (WITH OR WITHOUT PINEAPPLE)

Ingredients: 1 cup boiled macaroni

2 tblsp butter

2 tblsp maida (refined flour)

2 cups milk

½ tsp black pepper powder

1 tsp sugar

Salt to taste

1 cup cheese grated / shredded mozzarella

½ cup pineapple pieces (optional)

Method: 1) In a non-stick pan, heat butter and add maida and stir continuously, roast till you get an aroma.

2) Then slowly add milk and stir continuously such that no lumps are formed.

3) Then add pepper powder, salt and sugar and keep stirring till a thick white sauce is done.

4) Now add boiled macaroni and pineapple(if, using it)

5) Now put it in a greased pan and spread cheese on it

generously.

6) Bake in a pre-heated oven at 180° C till the cheese melts

and changes its colour.

VEG AUGRATIN LIP-SMACKING DISH

Ingredients: 50 gm butter

2 tsp maida (refined flour)

1 capsicum

1 carrot

1 potato (boiled)

50 gm palak (spinach) leaves

¼ cup boiled corn

¼ cup boiled green peas

½ cup boiled pasta

4 cheese cubes

½ litre milk

½ cup bread crumbs

1 tsp oregano

2 tsp chilli flakes

Method: 1) Take a pan, add butter, add maida and roast till you

get an aroma.

2) Add milk slowly and keep stirring to make thick white

sauce.

3) Add 1 cheese cube (grated), oregano and chilli flakes.

Mix well.

4) Add the veggies and mix slowly.

5) Take a flat bowl and grease it.

6) Then add this mix.

7) Spread bread crumbs and cheese on it.

8) Sprinkle oregano and chilli flakes.

9) Now bake in the pre-heated oven at 180° C till the

cheese melt or its colour changes .

10) Serve hot.

CHOLE ALOO PIE - ZARA HATKE

Ingredients: 1 cup chickpeas (chole) (soaked overnight and boiled)

1 tblsp oil

2 tsp ginger-garlic-chilli paste

½ cup tomato puree

½ cup onion paste

1 tsp red chilli powder

Salt to taste

1 tsp aamchur powder (dry mango powder)

½ tsp chole masala

6 large potatoes (boiled and mashed)

Pepper powder to taste

1 tblsp milk

1 tsp butter

1 cup grated mozzarella cheese

Method: 1) To prepare chole, take oil in a pan, add ginger-garlic

paste, onion paste and saute it.

2) Then add tomato puree and sauté for a minute.

3) Now add chilli powder, salt, aamchur, chole masala

and mix

4) Add 2-3 tblsp water if required & stir well. Keep chole

aside.

5) In a bowl, take mashed potatoes and add salt, pepper,

milk and butter to make like a paste.

6) In a greased baking dish, first make layer of chole,

then on it make a layer of potato paste.

7)On it spread cheese and put in a pre-heated oven at

200° C till the cheese melts.

8) Serve hot with tomato ketchup.

Tip: You can use rajma instead of chole.

KATHIYAWADI BRUSCHETTA - A FUSION RECIPE

Ingredients: 4 slices French loaf

1 tomato

8-9 garlic pods

1tblsp oil

Salt to taste

2 tblsp red chilli powder

1 onion (chopped finely)

2 tsp masala peanuts

Cheese as per liking

Butter for brushing the tray

Method: 1) Grind tomato, garlic, oil, salt and chilli powder to make a

fine paste.

2) Take the slices of French loaf bread and apply the garlic

paste on them.

3) Now put some onions, peanuts and cheese on each slice.

4) Now grease an oven tray and keep the bread on it and

bake it at 150° C till the cheese melts.

5) Serve hot with ketchup or green chutney.

Note: 1) You can use regular bread if French loaf is not available.

2) There is no need to pre-heat the oven in this recipe.

3) It can be prepared on a non-stick pan too.

LEMON CHEESE CAKE (NO BAKING REQUIRED)

Ingredients: 180gms cream cheese

200gms condensed milk

20 Marie biscuits

1 cup whipped cream

1 tblsp gelatin

3 tblsp melted butter

½ cup water

3 tblsp lemon juice

¼ lemon zest

Method: 1) Crush the biscuits and add butter to it and form a base for

the cheese cake. Refrigerate for 15 minutes.

2) Soak the gelatin in water and keep it aside.

3) In a bowl, whisk the cream cheese and condensed milk for

a few minutes.

4) Add the whipped cream gradually to the mixture of cream-

cheese and condensed milk.

5) Add lemon juice and lemon zest to it and mix well.

6) Take the soaked gelatin & dissolve it on low heat & let it

cool a little.

7) Add it to the cream mixture and pour it over the biscuit

base.

8) Refrigerate for about 6 hours, then serve chilled.

Tip: Decorate with cherries or any berries.

CUSTARD HALWA- MY STYLE

Ingredients: 200 ml milk

2 tblsp custard powder (dissolved in ½ cup milk)

4 tblsp sugar

1 tsp ghee

Sugar balls / nuts to garnish

Method: 1) Boil the milk with sugar.

2) When it boils, add the diluted custard powder and

stir continuously till it thickens a bit.

3) Finally add ghee and mix well.

4) Remove in a greased dish & sprinkle sugar balls or

nuts.

5) Cut into desired shapes, when cool.

6) Serve chilled.

MANGO MASTANI- SIMPLY MANGOLICIOUS!!!

Ingredients: 1 cup mango puree

½ cup milk

1 scoop vanilla ice-cream + 2 scoops vanilla ice-cream

1 tsp sugar (if required)

4 -5 ice-cubes

1 tblsp mango pieces

1 tblsp mixed nuts (chopped) [almonds, cashew nuts, raisins,

pistas]

Method: 1) Blend the mango puree, milk, 1 scoop of ice-cream, sugar and ice-cubes.

2) Pour in glasses and serve with a scoop of ice-cream,

mango pieces and nuts.

3) Serve chilled.

ROSE – COCONUT ICE-CREAM- COOL, COOL

Ingredients: 1litre milk

Sugar to taste

3 tblsp corn flour (dissolved in a cup of cold milk)

1 cup malai (cream)

4 tsp dessicated coconut

½ tsp rose water

½ tsp Rooh Afza or any Rose syrup

Method: 1) In a saucepan, take milk and sugar and boil.

2) When it boils, add dissolved corn flour and stir

continuously for about 8 – 10 minutes or till it thickens.

3) Let it cool down.

4) Now add cream, coconut, rosewater, rose syrup & mix

well.

5) Keep in an aluminium box with lid and set in the fridge.

6) After 5 – 6 hours, remove and churn again and then set

for another 5 – 6 hours.

7) Set until it is firm. Then serve.

Tip:		Garnish with rose petals.

CHOCO TART- RICH AND CHOCOLATY

Ingredients: 12 Marie biscuits

4 – 5 tblsp butter (melted) + 1 tsp butter

¼th slab dark chocolate (almost 100gm)

2 tblsp cream

2 tblsp powdered sugar

8 – 10 strawberries (cut into two)

Method: 1) Crush the biscuits to powder form, add butter and mix

well.

2) Take a loose bottom pie dish and put the mixture

evenly and tightly in it.

3) Refrigerate it for 15 minutes.

4) During this time, melt the chocolate in a double boiler

or microwave oven and add sugar, cream and 1tsp

butter and mix to prepare a ganache.

5) Now pour this ganache on the set layer of biscuits and

allow it to cool a little.

6) Decorate with strawberries cut into two and refrigerate

for an hour. Serve cold.

Tip: You can use white chocolate instead of dark chocolate.

FRUIT SALAD- UNUSUAL BUT DELICIOUS

Ingredients: 500 ml milk

2 tblsp custard powder (diluted in ½ cup cold milk)

4 tblsp sugar

1 banana (chopped)

1 chikoo (chopped)

5 – 6 grapes (cut into two)

½ apple (chopped)

1 tblsp mixed nuts (cashew nuts, almonds, pista etc)

Method: 1) Boil the milk

2) When it starts boiling, add sugar and stir well.

3) Then add the diluted custard powder and stir

continuously till the milk thickens a bit.

4) Remove from fire and allow it to cool.

5) When completely cool, add the fruits and
nuts and

refrigerate.

6) Serve chilled.

FRUIT CREAM- PERFECT COMBINATION!!

Ingredients:2 cups heavy dairy cream

3 tblsp icing sugar

2 rings pineapple (chopped)

1 ½ apple (chopped)

5 – 6 grapes (cut into two)

½ kiwi (chopped)

1 tblsp pomegranate seeds

Method: 1) Whip the cream with icing sugar till soft peaks form.

2) Mix all the fruits except pomegranate seeds.

3) Refrigerate for about 1 – 2 hours.

4) Serve chilled, garnished with pomegranate seeds.

Tip: Keep a tray of ice-cubes underneath the bowl of cream when you are whipping, to get the best results.

GULAB PHIRNI – Loved by all

Ingredients: 500ml milk (preferably full fat milk)

200gm rice

200gm sugar or according to taste

2 tblsp rose syrup

1tsp rose water

A few rose petals

Nuts (optional)

Method: 1) Soak the rice for an hour or more. Then make a thick

paste of it, using a little water.

2) Boil the milk. Then add sugar and rice paste to it and

continuously stir the mixture, on a low flame.

3) Now add the rose syrup, rose water and nuts. Stir

continuously till it turns thick.

4) Turn off the flame and let it cool completely. Then put it

in the fridge.

5) Garnish with rose petals or nuts and serve chilled.

Tip: You may add a few drops of edible red/pink colour, if you wish.

PEANUT SALAD- MAZEDAR

Ingredients: ¼ cup masala peanuts

½ cup onion (sliced)

1 tomato (chopped)

salt to taste

2 tblsp coriander leaves

Method: Take a bowl and mix all the ingredients and serve

immediately.

Tip: Add salt at the time of serving otherwise the salad will

become soggy.

RUSSIAN SALAD- Always welcome

Ingredients: 1½ cups fresh curds

1 small apple

50 gm pineapple

¼ cup pomegranate seeds

50 gm grapes

1 small cucumber (grated)

50 gm cabbage (shredded)

1 boiled and cubed potato

salt to taste

1 tsp black pepper powder

2 tsp powdered sugar

Method: 1) Tie the curds in a muslin cloth and hang it for about an

hour, to get thick hung curd.

2) Cut all the fruits in small pieces.

3) Squeeze the cucumber lightly to remove excess water.

Keep aside.

4) In a bowl, take hung curd and add all the fruits and

vegetables.

5) Add salt, pepper and sugar and mix well.

6) Serve chilled.

Tip:	Add salt and sugar at the time of serving.

CHICKPEA SALAD- PROTEIN-PACKED

Ingredients: 1 cup chickpeas

1 onion

1 tomato

1 capsicum

1 cup cabbage

½ carrot

salt to taste

1 tsp pepper powder

1 tblsp lemon juice

1 tsp olive oil

some pomegranate seeds

½ tsp chaat masala (optional)

Method : 1) Soak the chickpeas for 6 hours and then boil it with a little salt.

2) Finely chop all the vegetables.

3) In a bowl, mix all the vegetables, chickpeas and

pomegranate.

4) In a small bowl take olive oil, add lemon juice to it

with salt and pepper and mix well.

5) Add this dressing to the chickpea bowl and mix well.

6) Sprinkle chaat masala and serve.

Tip: This salad can be served chilled too.

BHINDI KADHI- DIFFERENT FROM THE REST

Ingredients: All ingredients of SWEET KADHI except jaggery

150 gms ladies finger (cut into small rounds)

salt to taste

½ tsp red chilli powder

¼ tsp turmeric powder

½ tsp dhania jeera powder

2 tblsp oil

Method: 1) Prepare the kadhi as per in SWEET KADHI without

using jaggery.

2) In a pan add oil and the ladies finger.

3) Cover and cook with all masalas done completely,

4) Now add ladies finger into the kadhi and mix well.

5) Bring this bhindi kadhi to boil again and serve hot with

rice or khichdi.

Tip: Instead of ladies finger, you can use brinjals, spring

onions, fenugreek (methi) leaves etc.

SWEET KADHI- MEETHI GUJARATI KADHI

Ingredients: 1 cup curds

3 tblsp besan (gram flour)

2 ½ tblsp jaggery

½ tsp mustard seeds

½ tsp cumin seeds

5 – 6 curry leaves

¼ tsp fenugreek seeds

a pinch of asafoetida

4 – 5 kokum

salt to taste

1 tblsp ginger-green chilli paste

½ cup coriander leaves

2 tblsp ghee

3 – 4 cloves

1 cinnamon stick

3 cups water

Method: 1) Whisk the curds and beat well with the besan and water.

2) Now in a saucepan, transfer the beaten mixture and

stir continuously.

3) Add jaggery, kokum, salt, ginger-chilli paste and keep

stirring for 5-7 minutes.

4) Then in a separate pan take ghee, add mustard seeds,

cumin seeds, fenugreek seeds, curry leaves and asafoetida.

Let it splutter.

5) Then add cloves and cinnamon and pour this baghar in

the boiling kadhi and keep stirring for another 2 minutes.

6) Garnish with coriander leaves and serve hot with rice or

khichdi

SINDHI KADHI- MUST TRY!!!

Ingredients: ½ cup besan (gram flour)

2 tblsp oil

2 cups cut vegetables (drumsticks, ladies finger, guvar,

potatoes, sweet gourd etc.)

¼ cup chopped tomatoes

1 lemon juice

salt to taste

1 tsp fenugreek seeds

½ tsp mustard seeds

½ tsp cumin seeds

½ tsp red chilli powder

½ tsp turmeric powder

1 tsp dhania jeera powder

2 tblsp chopped coriander leaves

water as required

Method:	1) In a vessel, take oil and add mustard seeds, fenugreek

seeds, cumin seeds and allow to splutter.

2) Then add the besan and roast till the besan changes

its colour slightly and becomes aromatic.

3) Then add the cut vegetables, salt, turmeric, red chilli

powder, dhania jeera powder and mix well.

4) Then add water enough to cook the vegetables.

5) Cover and cook on medium flame till all vegetables

are cooked. (You can add water, as required)

6) Now add tomatoes, lemon juice & Stir well for 2

minutes.

7) Add coriander leaves and serve hot with rice.

DAL MAKHANI- TOO MAKHANI

Ingredients: 100 gms kidney beans (rajma) [soaked for 6 – 7 hours]

100 gms masoor (whole) [soaked for 6 – 7 hours]

2 tblsp ghee

1 tblsp butter

2 onions (finely chopped)

1 tblsp garlic paste

4 tomatoes (grated)

2 tsp garam masala

salt to taste

1 tsp coriander leaves

1 tsp kasuri methi (dried fenugreek leaves)

Method: 1) Boil the rajma and masoor for 6 – 7 whistles so that they are cooked well. Add a pinch of salt while boiling.

2) Heat ghee in a vessel and add onions and garlic paste

and saute for 3 – 4 minutes.

3) Now add the tomatoes and cook for another 2

minutes.

4) Add a little water to it and boil the gravy.

5) Now add the boiled pulses, salt and garam masala

and mix well.

6) If required you can add a little water but be careful

not to make it runny.

7) Let it simmer for 7 – 8 minutes, then add butter to it.

8) Garnish with coriander and kasuri methi and serve hot

with parathas or rice.

KHATI- MEETHI DAL (GUJARATI STYLE)

Ingredients: 1cup tuver dal (boiled and mashed)

2 tblsp oil

¼ tsp mustard seeds

¼ tsp cumin seeds

4 – 5 curry leaves

¼ tsp fenugreek seeds

1 dry red chilli

a pinch of asafoetida

2 tblsp jaggery

1 lemon juice

½ tsp groundnuts

3 – 4 kokum (soaked in water)

salt to taste

1 tsp red chilli powder

¼ tsp turmeric powder

½ tsp kitchen king masala or garam masala powder

1 tsp dhania jeera powder

water as required

coriander leaves to garnish

1 tomato (finely chopped)

Method: 1) In a sauce pan, take oil, add cumin deeds, mustard

seeds, fenugreek seeds, curry leaves, dry chilli,

asafoetida and saute till the seeds splutter.

2) Add the dal and 2 cups water & add jaggery,

groundnuts, tomatoes, kokum & all the masalas. Mix &

boil for few minutes.

3) Finally add lemon juice and serve hot garnished with

coriander leaves. Serve with plain rice.

DAL FRY- HEALTH BHI TASTE BHI

Ingredients: 1cup tuver dal

½ cup chana dal

½ cup masoor dal

½ cup moong dal

1 cup urad dal

2 tblsp ghee

a pinch of asafoetida

1 tsp cumin seeds

4 onions (finely chopped)

10 cloves garlic (chopped)

5 green chillies (paste)

4 tomatoes (puree)

1 tsp red chilli powder

1 tsp dhania jeera powder

1 tsp garam masala

salt to taste

1 inch ginger (paste)

coriander leaves for garnish

Method: 1) Boil the dals but do not mash them once they are

cooked.

2) Heat the ghee and fry cumin seeds and add

asafoetida.

3) Now add onions, fry for 2 minutes.

4) Then add garlic, ginger and chilli paste and fry for a

minute.

5) Now add tomato puree and cook for 2 – 3 minutes.

6) Add cooked dals & all the masalas & simmer for 5

minutes.

7) Remove from flame and garnish with coriander leaves.

PALAK PURI- GO GREEN

Ingredients: 200 gms spinach (blanched and pureed)

2 tblsp green chilli paste

2 cups wheat flour

2 tblsp ghee

salt to taste

oil for frying

Method: 1) Take the wheat flour and add all ingredients except oil.

2) Mix and knead into a not-so soft dough.

3) Divide the dough into small balls and roll them into

puris.

4) Deep fry them in hot oil and serve hot.

Tip: You can add a tblsp of sooji (rava) if you want.

SHAHI BIRYANI - REALLY ROYAL!

Ingredients: 1 cup basmati rice (soaked for 2 hours)

10 cashew nuts

15 raisins

6 almonds

10 groundnuts

a few strands of saffron soaked in 1 tbslp milk

For the gravy: 20 gms ginger

10 garlic cloves

5 cloves

3 cinnamon sticks

¼ tsp coriander seeds

100 gms onions (paste)

2 tsp garam masala

1 tsp dhania jeera powder

¼ tsp turmeric

100 gms tomato ketchup

1 tsp salt

5 red chillies (dried)

2 tblsp oil

Method: <u>For the red paste</u>:1)Take ginger, chillies, garlic, cinnamon,

cloves, coriander seeds and cumin seeds and make a fine paste.

2) Heat oil (1 tblsp) and fry the paste for 2 minutes.

3) Add onion paste and fry again for 2 minutes.

4) Add all the other ingredients and fry till the masalas

become brown.

5) Add the ketchup and a little water and cook for another

5 minutes. In this way, the red gravy is ready.

6) Boil the rice and cook the rice only 80% and strain the water.

7) Keep the rice aside.

8) Heat 1 tblsp ghee and fry the cashewnuts, raisins,

almonds and groundnuts and keep aside.

9) Mix the rice and nuts with saffron milk and salt, such that

the grains do not break. Then mix the red gravy and toss

the rice.

10) Cover the lid and cook for 2 minutes. Serve hot.

MIX DAL SPICY KHICHDI -A SURE SHOT

Ingredients: 1cup tuver dal (soaked)

1 cup rice (soaked)

1 potato (cubed)

1 tomato (cubed)

1 onion (cubed)

½ capsicum (cubed)

salt to taste

2 tblsp ghee

2 cloves

2 cardamom

1 cinnamon stick

¼ tsp cumin seeds

¼ tsp mustard seeds

¼ tsp fenugreek seeds

3 – 4 curry leaves

1 dry red chilli

½ tsp turmeric powder

1 tsp red chilli powder

3 cups of water

Method: 1) In a cooker, put the ghee, add mustard seeds, cumin

seeds, fenugreek seeds, curry leaves, dry chilli and

garam masala and prepare the tempering (baghar).

2) Now add the vegetables and mix.

3) Then add the rice and dal and the salt, turmeric

powder, chilli powder and mix well.

4) Add the water, close the lid and cook for 3 whistles.

5) Let the cooker cool on its own. Then serve the

khichdi with ghee

FRIED RICE- DESI CHINESE

Ingredients: 500 gm rice (soaked for 2 hours)

2 tblsp oil

a pinch of citric acid

100 gm french beans (finely chopped)

100 gm carrots (finely chopped)

3 spring onions (finely chopped)

a pinch of aji-no-moto (optional)

1 capsicum (finely chopped)

1 tsp soya sauce

½ tsp black pepper powder

1 tsp vinegar

salt to taste

Method: 1) Cook the rice and strain the water. Keep aside the rice.

2) Par boil the french beans and drain the water and

keep aside.

3) Heat the oil and add the vegetables & aji-no-moto.

Cook on a high flame for 3 to 4 minutes.

4) Add salt, soya sauce, pepper, vinegar and rice. Mix

well and cook for 2 minutes.

5) Garnish with green spring onions and serve hot.

VEG. PULAV-HEALTHY

Ingredients: 1 cup basmati rice

100 gms potatoes (cut into small pieces)

100 gms French beans (cut into small pieces)

100 gms carrots (cut into small pieces)

100 gms green peas

2 tblsp ghee

1 tsp cumin seeds

2 pieces cinnamon sticks

6 cloves

4 green chillies (finely chopped)

a small piece ginger (finely chopped)

¼ tsp turmeric powder

1 tsp garam masala

salt to taste

Method: 1) Soak the rice for 2 hours. Then boil it till it is 70 – 80 %

cooked. Drain the water and keep aside.

2) Boil the vegetables and keep aside.

3) Heat ghee in a pan, add cumin seeds, cloves &

cinnamon sticks.

4) Then add green chillies, ginger and turmeric powder.

5) Mix and add all the vegetables and saute for 2

minutes.

6) Now add the salt and garam masala and mix well.

7) Now add the rice, mix carefully, so that the grains do

not break.

8) Cover the lid and cook for 5 – 7 minutes on low flame.

9) Serve hot with any raita or plain curds.

LACHCHA PARATHA (EASIEST WAY)

Ingredients: 1 cup wheat flour + 3 tblsp dry wheat flour

1 tsp oil

¼ tsp salt

4 tsp ghee for applying + 2 tsp for frying

water for kneading the dough

Method: 1) Take 1 cup wheat flour, add oil and salt and knead a soft

dough with little water. Keep aside for 10 minutes.

2) Now make 4 balls from the dough and roll out rotis, with

the help of dry wheat flour.

3) Now apply ghee on each roti and sprinkle dry wheat

flour on it.

4) Now start folding the roti like a hand fan (one fold on the

other)

5) Now roll the folded roti into a bun and press a little.

6) Again roll the roti with the help of dry wheat flour.

7) Now roast the rotis and fry them with the help of ghee.

8) Each roti will have layers.

9) Serve hot with ghee applied on it.

Tip: You can use refined flour (maida) instead of wheat flour.

MASALA PARATHA-NAMKEEN

Ingredients: <u>For the stuffing</u>:

1 cup leftover namkeen (chivda, sev, chavana etc.)

½ tsp dry mango powder (aamchur powder)

½ tsp chaat masala

½ tsp red chilli powder

Handful of coriander leaves

<u>For the dough</u>:

1 cup wheat flour + 3 tblsp wheat flour

¼ tsp salt

1 tsp oil

water for kneading the dough

ghee for frying

Method: 1) Take the left over namkeen and grind it to make a paste.

2) Now add dry mango powder, chaat masala, red chilli

powder and coriander leaves and mix with the paste.

Keep aside.

3) Knead the dough with wheat flour, salt, oil and water.

4) Make 4 balls from it and roll out the rotis.

5) Now take some stuffing and put on the rotis, then gather

the side and make like a ball and roll it again into a roti.

6) Now heat a girdle and fry the rotis with the help of ghee.

7) Serve hot with curds or any raita of your choice.

BUTTER NAAN- DIRECT PUNJAB SE

Ingredients: 4 cups refined flour

1 tsp baking powder

¼ cup milk

2 tblsp curds

1 tsp sugar

1 tsp dry yeast + ¾ cup luke warm water

2 tsp melted ghee

butter

salt to taste

Method: 1) Sieve the maida, baking powder and salt. Keep aside.

2) Heat milk, add sugar and yeast to it. Dissolve them & add the flour after 10 minutes. Knead into a hard dough.

3) Mix curds with the dough and knead well again.

4) Add ghee and knead till the dough is soft.

5) Keep the dough under a wet cloth for 4 – 5 hours.

6) Make lemon size balls from it & apply little ghee on

them.

7) Cover the balls with wet cloth for 15 – 20 minutes.

8) Apply a little ghee to the rolling pin and roll out the

naans.

9) Apply little water on one side of the naan and paste it

on the hot griddle.

10) After a few seconds, place the griddle upside down

on the gas.

11) When naan is roasted apply butter and serve hot.

Tip: After rolling the naan, sprinkle a few kalonji seeds on it, press

slightly and roll again.

METHI DHEBRA OR PURI- WINTER SPECIAL

Ingredients: 250 gm bajri flour

50 gms wheat flour

250 gms fenugreek (methi) leaves (finely chopped)

½ cup coriander leaves (finely chopped)

50 gm garlic paste

2 tblsp sesame seeds

1 tsp red chilli powder

2 tblsp jaggery powder

½ tsp ajwain (carom seeds)

4 green chillies (finely chopped)

salt to taste

a pinch of asafoetida

oil for frying

Method: 1) Mix all ingredients except oil and knead a dough.

2) Divide the dough into small balls.

3) Roll out each ball into a thick roti.

4) Using a cookie cutter, cut into small roundels.

5) Roast the puri on the griddle using oil to make dhebra or

fry it to make puri.

6) Serve with any pickle or chutney.

SIMPLE PLAIN ROTI- BASIC RECIPE

Ingredients: 1 cup wheat flour + 3 tblsp dry wheat flour

1 tsp oil

¼ tsp salt

water for kneading the dough

ghee to apply on the rotis

Method:1) Take wheat flour in a mixing bowl and add oil, salt to it &

mix well.

2) Take water, little by little, and knead a soft dough. Keep

aside for about 15 minutes.

3) Make small balls of the dough & roll out the rotis.

4) On a hot girdle, roast the rotis till done on both sides.

5) Apply ghee on the rotis and serve.

Tip: You can also puff the rotis on the gas after lightly roasting on

the girdle.

TAVA MEHFIL- WEDDING FAVOURITE

Ingredients: <u>For the stuffing</u>: 2 tsp coriander seeds

2 tsp cumin seeds

2 whole dry chillies

½ tsp fenugreek seeds

½ tsp asafoetida

1 tsp mustard seeds

1 tsp red chilli powder

2 tblsp peanuts

2 tsp sesame seeds

2 tblsp garam masala

½ tsp turmeric powder

1 tblsp aamchur powder

1 tsp chaat masala

1 tsp sugar

salt to taste

For the Gravy: 1 tsp caraway seeds (ajwain)

2 onions (finely chopped)

2 tblsp ginger-garlic paste

2 tomatoes (finely chopped)

2 tbslp oil

water as required

Vegetables required: 6 baby potatoes (slit halfway)

10 ladies finger (slit halfway)

8 small brinjal (slit halfway)

6 big fat green chillies/jalepenos (slit halfway)

6 parwal (slit halfway)

50 gms paneer (cut into finger-like cubes)

Method: 1) Dry roast coriander seeds, cumin seeds, dry chillies,

fenugreek, mustard, asafoetida, peanuts and sesame.

2) When roasted and cool, add turmeric, red chilli

powder, salt, sugar, garam masala, aamchur, chaat masala and dry grind into powder form.

3) Now stuff all the vegetables with this powder and shallow fry them one by one.

4) Take another pan in which you can cook and serve

this recipe.

5) Add a little oil and caraway seeds.

6) Now add onions, ginger-garlic paste and saute for a

minute.

7) Now add tomatoes and the extra powder left after

stuffing the vegetables.

8) Add a little water and mix well.

9) Now bring this masala in the middle of the pan and

arrange the cooked vegetables on the sides of the pan.

10) Keep the flame low all the time and serve the

vegetables of people's choice with the masala.

SEV-TOMATO SABJI- KATHIYAWADI STYLE

Ingredients:250 gms tomatoes (chopped into big pieces)

2 tblsp oil

½ tsp mustard seeds

½ tsp cumin seeds

1 tsp red chilli powder

1 tsp dhania-jeera powder

½ tsp turmeric powder

1 tsp garam masala

salt to taste

1 tblsp jaggery

100 gm thick sev

Method: 1) Heat oil for seasoning. Add mustard seeds and cumin

seeds. Allow to splutter.

2) Then add tomatoes, jaggery and all the masalas. Mix well.

3) Add a little water and allow to simmer for 5 minutes.Sabji

is ready.

4) While serving, add the sev and serve hot.

ONION – PAPAD SABJI- MONSOON MUST

Ingredients:4 papads (cut into medium size pieces)

2 tblsp oil

½ tsp cumin seeds

a pinch of asafoetida

100 gms spring onions (finely chopped)

1 tsp dhana-jeera powder

1 tsp red chilli powder

½ tsp turmeric powder

salt to taste

1 cup of water

Method: 1) Heat oil in a vessel and add cumin seeds. Let it splutter.

2) Then add papad pieces.

3) Add 1 cup of water, spring onions and cook for 5 minutes.

4) Add all the masalas. Cook for a minute.

5) Serve hot.

Tip: If spring onions are not available, use regular onions.

BAINGAN BHARTA- WINTER SPECIAL RECIPE

Ingredients: 250 large brinjal (bhutta)

2 tblsp oil

2 tsp ghee

1 tsp cumin seeds

a pinch of asafoetida (hing)

¼ tsp turmeric powder

1 tsp red chilli powder

200 gms onions (finely chopped)

10 cloves garlic (finely chopped)

100 gms tomatoes (finely chopped)

1 lime juice

1 tblsp ginger-chilli paste

1 tsp garam masala powder

salt to taste

2 tblsp coriander leaves

Method: 1) Apply a little oil to the brinjal and roast it on the gas,

turning it at frequent intervals.

2) When roasted well, remove its skin and mash it well.

3) Heat oil and ghee in a pan, add asafoetida, turmeric, red

chilli powder, onions and garlic. Saute it for a few minutes.

4) Add tomatoes and continue to saute it.

5) Now add mashed brinjal, salt, lime juice, ginger-chilli

paste and garam masala and mix well.

6) Cook a few minutes & serve hot.

7) Garnish with coriander leaves.

DAHI BHINDI- THE BEST BHINDI SABJI

Ingredients: 300 gms bhindi (okra /lady's finger)

1 onion (finely chopped)

2 green chillies (finely chopped)

1 tblsp garlic (crushed)

½ tsp red chilli powder

4 tblsp curds

1 tsp mustard seeds

1 tsp cumin seeds

1 tsp fennel seeds

salt to taste

1 tsp aamchur powder (dry mango powder)

3 tblsp oil

2 tomatoes (finely chopped)

Method: 1) Cut the bhindi in long thin slices and cook them in 2

tblsp oil adding turmeric, red chilli powder and salt.

Keep aside.

2) Add 1 tblsp oil in the same pan. Add mustard, cumin

and fennel seeds and allow to splutter.

3) Now add onions, green chillies and garlic and saute it

till onions soften a bit.

4) Then add tomatoes and cook till they also soften.

5) Now add curds and bhindi and mix well.

6) Cook a little for about 5 minutes.

7) Serve hot with roti.

SIMPLE POTATO SABJI- VERY SIMPLE

Ingredients: 3 potatoes (cubed)

1 tomato (cubed)

1 tblsp oil

½ tsp mustard seeds

½ tsp cumin seeds

a few curry leaves

¼ tsp fenugreek seeds (methi dana)

a pinch of asafoetida (hing)

salt to taste

¼ tsp turmeric powder

1 tsp red chilli powder

½ tsp dhania-jeera powder

2 tblsp coriander leaves

½ cup water

Method: 1) In a cooker, put oil and add mustard, cumin and

fenugreek seeds. Allow to splutter.

2) Now add asafoetida and curry leaves.

3) Then add the potatoes and tomatoes and stir a little.

4) Now add salt, red chilli powder, turmeric powder,

dhania-jeera powder and ½ cup water. Mix well.

5) Close the lid and cook for 2 – 3 whistles.

6) When cool open the lid and serve garnished with

coriander leaves.

VEGETABLE BALLS- VITAMIN LOADED

Ingredients:4 boiled and mashed potatoes

150 gm spring onions finely chopped

100 gm green peas (boiled)

1 small carrot finely chopped

cheese cubes (optional)

4 tblsp bread crumbs

½ tsp turmeric powder

1 tblsp aamchur powder

1 tsp red chilli powder

1 tsp sesame seeds

1 inch ginger

2 tblsp coriander leaves

1 tblsp chaat masala

salt to taste

1 tblsp corn flour diluted in a little water for slurry

oil to fry

Method: 1) In a mixing bowl take potatoes, spring onions, green peas, carrot, turmeric powder, aamchur, red chilli powder, sesame seeds, ginger pieces, coriander leaves, chaat masala and salt and mix well and make small balls. Keep aside.

2) Take the balls one by one and dip in the slurry.

3) Roll them one by one in the bread crumbs & deep fry.

Serve hot.

POTATO CHEESE BALLS-
EVERYONE'S CHOICE

Ingredients: 500 gms boiled potatoes

2 cups grated mozzarella cheese

3 green chillies

1 finely chopped onion

½ cup bread crumbs

salt to taste

black pepper powder to taste

oil to fry

Method: 1) Take a bowl and mash the boiled potatoes.

2) Add salt, pepper and bread crumbs and knead a dough.

3) Now prepare the stuffing. Take onions. Add salt, pepper,

chillies and cheese to it and mix well.

4) Make small balls from the potato mixture and stuff it with

a smaller ball of the stuffing, properly.

5) Now keep the stuffed balls in the fridge for about 15

minutes.

6) Then deep fry the balls in hot oil till golden brown.

7) Serve hot.

Tip: You can also add corn to the stuffing.

HARA BHARA KEBAB- MANPASAND

Ingredients:1 bunch of spinach (finely chopped)

½ cup green peas (boiled)

2 potatoes (big)

¼ cup coriander leaves

¼ cup   mint leaves (optional)

½ cup bread crumbs

1 tblsp green chilli and ginger paste

1 tsp aamchur powder

1 tsp chaat masala

1 tsp cumin powder

salt to taste

oil   to   shallow fry

Method: 1) Boil the potatoes, peel and mash them. Keep aside.

2) Blanch the spinach and keep aside.

3) Now take a bowl and mix all ingredients except oil.

4) Give a proper shape to the cutlets from the mixture.

5) In a non-stick pan, shallow fry them in oil.

6) Serve hot with a dip of your choice.

COCONUT AND PEANUT- SOUP UNIQUE!!

Ingredients: 1 cup coconut milk

1 tblsp peanuts (roasted)

1 tblsp sweet corn kernels (boiled)

1 tblsp finely chopped capsicum

$\frac{1}{4}$ tsp oregano

$\frac{1}{4}$ tsp chilli flakes

$\frac{1}{2}$ tsp sugar

1 tsp cornflour (optional)

Salt to taste

Water as required

Method: 1) Pulse grind the peanuts to fine powder. Keep aside.

2) In a sauce pan, pour the milk with little water and bring to

boil.

3) Add the other ingredients one by one and stir continuously.

4) Bring to boil till you get the desired consistency. (Add

diluted corn flour only if the soup is very runny)

5) Enjoy it hot.

CHILLI BEAN SOUP- SIMPLY DELICIOUS

Ingredients: 100gm red beans

2 tsp oil

2 spring onions (finely chopped)

1 capsicum (finely chopped)

1 onion (finely chopped)

500gm tomatoes

2 tsp sugar

¼ tsp red chilli powder

Salt to taste

Grated cheese for garnish

Method: 1) Soak the beans in hot water overnight and cook till

done.

2) Cut the tomatoes into big pieces, add about 3 cups of

water and cook.]Then squeeze through a sieve to get

the soup.

3) Heat oil in a vessel and add all the veggies and sauté for

2 minutes.

4) Now add the tomato soup and boil for a few minutes.

5) Add the beans, salt and sugar. Cook for a few minutes.

6) Serve hot with grated cheese.

Tip: You can use the tinned baked beans, if you desire.

BROCCOLI ALMOND SOUP- HOT FAVOURITE

Ingredients: 3 cups broccoli (cut into florets)

1 onion (sliced)

4 cloves garlic (finely chopped)

1 cup milk

¼ cup almonds (peeled)

1 tsp olive oil

Salt to taste

Black pepper powder to taste

Method: 1) Take a pan and heat oil on medium heat.

2) Add garlic and onion and sauté till the onions soften.

3) Add broccoli and sauté it for a minute.

4) Add salt, cover the pan and cook for about 3 minutes.

5) Allow to cool. Now grind the broccoli mixture with almonds

and make a smooth puree.

6) Now add milk and bring to boil. Turn off the gas.

7) Sprinkle pepper powder and serve hot.

SAGO SOUP-TOTALLY DIFFERENT

Ingredients: 2 tsp sago (washed properly)

1 maggi seasoning cube

1 small onion (peeled and sliced)

1 carrot (peeled and cut into thin strips)

4 cups water

¼ tsp black pepper powder

1 tsp lime juice

1 tsp soya sauce

½ tsp sugar

Salt to taste

Coriander leaves to garnish

Method: 1) Mix water, seasoning cube and sago and boil till sago is

cooked.

2) Add onions and carrots and continue boiling for 5 minutes.

3) Add salt, pepper, sugar and lime juice.

4) When soup thickens to your liking, add soya sauce and

coriander leaves and serve hot.

Tip: Instead of water & seasoning cube, you can use 4 cups

vegetable stock.

SPINACH SOUP- GREEN AND HEALTHY

Ingredients: 250 gm spinach (washed and roughly chopped)

150 gm green peas (shelled)

2 onions (peeled and roughly chopped)

6 cloves garlic

1½ tsp sugar

2 tblsp corn flour

A pinch of baking soda

A pinch of nutmeg powder

A pinch of white pepper powder

4 tblsp cream

Salt to taste

3 ½ glasses of water

Method: 1) Boil 3 glasses of water and when it starts boiling, add spinach and onions.

2) After a minute add garlic, sugar, peas, salt and soda and

boil for 5 minutes with the lid on. Cool the mixture and

blend it.

3) Now, sieve it with a strainer and keep again on the gas

stove.

4) Dissolve corn flour in ½ glass water and pour it in the

boiling soup.

5) Add nutmeg powder and pepper powder and stir

continuously till you get the desired consistency.

6) Serve hot with cream as garnish.

RED SOUP- DIL SE

Ingredients: 2 big beetroots

1 big carrot

1 tomato

1-2 glasses water

Salt to taste

½ tsp. black pepper powder

2-3 mint leaves

Method: 1) Peel the beetroots and carrot.

2) Cut all the vegetables into cubes.

3) Put them in a pressure cooker with salt, pepper and

water.

4) Pressure cook till 4 whistles and let the cooker cool

down.

5) Now blend the boiled veggies and pour in the soup

bowls.

6) Garnish with mint leaves and serve hot.

Tip: Before garnishing and serving, you can sieve the soup with a

strainer, if you like.

Appendix

<u>Weights and Measures</u>

1 teaspoon (tsp) = 5 ml

1 tablespoon (tblsp) = 15 ml

OR

1 tablespoon (tblsp) = 3 teaspoons (tsp)

1 cup = 210ml OR 1 cup = 16 tblsp

1 kilo = 2 ½ pounds

1 litre = 1000 ml

Certain food items can be easily measured by a measuring cup. For e.g. 250gm of the following food items equals to different measurement in cup.

Refined flour (Maida) = 2 cups

Rice = 1 cup

Sugar = 1 cup

Icing sugar = 1¾ cup

Butter = 1 cup

Paneer (Cottage cheese) = 1 cup

Grated cheese = 2 cups

Cream = 1 cup

<u>Oven Temperature chart for baking</u>

° F	OR	_°C
225		110
250		125
275		140
300		150
325		165
350		180
375		195
400		210

<u>TIPS TO KEEP IN MIND WHILE BAKING</u>

1. The baking time and temperature differs from oven to oven. It very much depends on the dish's size or weight.

2. Pre-heating the oven is a very important step in baking. It keeps the over ready in advance, at the temperature at which the food is to be cooked so that

food is cooked evenly.

3. Always allow baked cakes, cookies or bread to rest before you try to cut it or eat it. Giving rest time allows proper slicing or getting a proper crunch etc.

4. Always use proper mittens or a thick cloth to remove hot baked food from the oven to avoid burning of hands.

5. Do not clean the oven when hot. Let it cool down completely before you do so.

Glossary

BRINJAL – BAINGAN
PATTA GOBI

CABBAGE –

CARROT – GAJAR
BEANS – GUVAR

CLUSTER

CORIANDER – DHANIA
LEAVES - KADHIPATTA

CURRY

DRUMSTICKS – SAHAJAN
CUCUMBER - KHIRA

ENGLISH

FENUGREEK – METHI
LEHSUN

GARLIC –

GINGER – ADRAK
PEAS – MATAR

GREEN

LADY'S FINGER – BHINDI
CHILLI – HARI MIRCH

GREEN

POMEGRANATE – ANAR
ALOO

POTATO –

SWEET GOURD – LAUKI
PALAK

SPINACH –

RAW MANGO – KERI

KIDNEY BEANS – RAJMA

PEANUTS/GROUND NUTS – SING

CHICKPEA – CHOLE

MUSTARD SEEDS – SARSON

CUMIN SEEDS – JEERA

FENNEL SEEDS – SAUNF

JAGGERY – GUD

BLACK PEPPER – KALI MIRCH

NUTMEG – JAIPHAL

POPPY SEEDS – AFEEM KE BEEJ

CINNAMON – TUJ

CLOVES – LAUNG

CARDAMOM- ELAICHI

ALMOND – BAADAM

CASHEWNUTS – KAJU

RAISINS – KISMIS

ASAFOETIDA – HING

DRY MANGO POWDER – AAMCHUR

TURMERIC – HALDI

CARAWAY SEEDS – AJWAIN

SESAME SEEDS – TIL

GREEN GRAM – MOONG

GRAMFLOUR – BESAN

REFINED FLOUR – MAIDA   RED LENTIL – MASOOR

CITRIC ACID – NIMBU KE PHOOL   VINEGAR – SIRKA

DRY FENUGREEK LEAVES – KASURI METHI

COTTAGE CHEESE – PANEER   MILLET – BAJRI

DESSICATED COCONUT – NARIYEL KA BURADA

ROSE WATER – GULABJAL   SAFFRON – ZAFRAN (KESAR)

AJI-NO-MOTO – SODIUM GLUTAMATE

Notes

USER'S NOTES: